Maxyne Gaelynn Bursky
BA, RPR, CCR, CRR

TALK TO THE HANDS!

A practical guide for the new court reporter, with tips on how to hit the ground running in this fabulous field – without actually hitting the ground!

TALK TO THE HANDS!

By Maxyne Gaelynn Bursky

Copyright© 2011 by Maxyne Gaelynn Bursky

Cover art copyright© 2011 by Maxyne G. Bursky

Photographs by Jena Golden Photography

Cover design by Kip Williams, Print-Ink Press

Have a question about reporting? Contact Maxyne at
TalkToTheHands1K@aol.com or
on our Facebook page, Talk to the Hands 1K

ISBN: 978-0-9821555-1-6
0-9821555-1-4

Dedicated to Richie, my soulmate, and the best court reporting mentor that anyone could have.

Table of Contents

Introduction

The first thing to understand about this book is that this is NOT a bunch of academic exercises that, once mastered, will get you a passing grade on a test, or a certificate from a state or national organization. You will NOT hear most of what is in this book from any teacher, as they are more concerned with getting you up to speed literally, cramming you full of medical and legal terminology, and making sure you go out into the world of litigation as close to achieving 100 percent accuracy as possible.

Talk to the Hands is a practical approach to court reporting as it takes place out in the work environment, whether it be in court, at an attorney's office, or even at conventions and conferences. After reading through this, you will be equipped to step into a trial or deposition from the get-go as if you had years of field experience under your belt. Of course, experience counts for a great deal in this business, but you will attain a level of professional maturity that much faster by incorporating some of these suggestions from the beginning.

If you are reading these words, I assume you are just chomping at the bit, eager to get to work and start earning a living in a profession that has promised you a comfortable return on the big bucks you paid in to court reporting school. You can do as I did, jumping headlong into the legal world and working as a reporter the old-fashioned way, profiting from knowledge gained often as a result of stressful experiences for which I was not prepared, or you can choose to benefit from the lessons us "old horses" have learned and, from the beginning, create a job that you wake up every morning, eager to enjoy.

There is no right or wrong when it comes to the tips that you will get in this book. All suggestions are completely within the guidelines of quality and accuracy and professionalism that are promulgated by the NCRA (National Court Reporters Association), and the NVRA (National Voice Writers Association), although these organizations have not officially endorsed this publication. Some ideas may seem like everyday common sense; yet others may feel too radical or uncomfortable for you to implement, or you don't feel quite ready to tackle certain issues in the time frame I advocate.

The beauty of these concepts is that they are merely helpful hints, practical approaches to sometimes stringent and orthodox requirements. Keep reminding yourself that as you turn the pages, if it doesn't apply, let it fly. Just go on to the next chapter and see what you can use. But if something in here resonates with you, highlight it, star it, dog-ear the page. It will serve you in the months and years to come.

Although I have spent some time working in court, the majority of my career has been as a freelance reporter, so some of the ideas you will read here may not apply to in-court work. For example, in one chapter I recommend premarking exhibit stickers before the start of a deposition; in court, the clerk marks the exhibits. So if you are headed for the courtroom as an official, simply skip that offering and go on to those that work best for you.

Just one more thing: Don't worry about retaining every point made here that you feel can benefit you. Just as it took time, tremendous effort, and focus to become comfortable with the mechanical requirements of this most unusual and distinctive profession, it will take time to internalize the ideas in this book.

When you first took the wheel, driving was an exciting but at the same time frequently overwhelming process, with all the details to remember; and now there are times when you get to your destination and can't remember how you got there.

Your new court reporting habits will soon become natural and fluid. Welcome to a greatly rewarding and exciting career!

1
Cheat Sheets Are Sweet!

In over 30 years of reporting, there is one habit I have clung to that has served me well. I maintain a spiral notebook filled with the steps I need to follow when a procedure that is new to me shows up. Times have changed radically since I started this job with a mechanical steno machine and a paper tape, and copies of transcripts were created by a typist operating a manual typewriter using carbon sheets surrounded by flimsy paper. The computer age has definitely touched our profession in exciting and challenging ways.

The drawback for me was frequently needing to become familiar with new processes that were very different from what I was used to. My solution was to keep a "cheat notebook," a sort of journal in which I detailed how I was to operate my equipment. I numbered each and every step, from opening my computer, to connecting it to my retooled steno machine, to shutting it all down at the end of the assignment. It may have seemed elementary to other reporters (all of whom appeared to know what they were doing from the starting gate), but my learning curve is much longer, and I need to plod along slowly until it feels right to me.

I never showed the notebook to anyone, but took it with me to every deposition, every trial. When first asked to give a realtime feed of the raw transcript that was appearing on my computer to an attorney in a deposition, I happily opened my notebook to the page for realtime setup and followed the steps I had written out.

Don't be concerned that the lawyers in the room will see the notebook and say (or even think), "Aren't you familiar with this? You need to follow instructions?" In all the time that I have used this tool, no one has ever commented to that effect, nor has anyone ever called my office and complained that, "The court reporter did a great job, but she was reading from a notebook!"

On the job, I am always prepared to reply, "I'm sorry, I am *such* a perfectionist that I like to double- and triple-check my procedures." Remember, you are working with a group of professionals who pray to the god of preparation. Lawyers fully understand what it means to have all your ducks in a row. So, just for security, feel free to squeeze in a few more ducks!

Bytes are beautiful. All of us in this WiFi society are married to our computers. One of the great teachers of this generation of verbatim professionals is the feedback we receive from our software. In most cases, barring technical problems, the quality of whatever efforts we put into creating our transcripts is immediately reflected back to us on the screen of our cyber-pal. If our writing is sloppy, if we are having a bad day, missteps will show up as words either untranslated or mistranslated in the body of the unedited transcript.

My response to that is, how fabulous! You get immediate, visual cues that signal that you have a lazy pinkie on your right hand and your final **T** is showing up as final **TS** and you are creating unwanted plurals or even complete misstrokes. For those who are voice writers, you may not be speaking clearly enough and what is showing up on the screen is not at all what you just dictated into your mask.

These kinds of errors give you the chance to concentrate on cleaning up your reporting in these areas as you continue practicing (see Chapter 5).

Don't worry. A favorite expression of mine is, "I was given an opportunity to screw up, and I took it!" It is not a just a jaded phrase to acknowledge that we learn from our mistakes. Indeed, how fabulous. The important thing is to work hard to keep those opportunities to a reasonable minimum!

What I also like to do is use a sort of "computer cheat" program that is a marvelous part of my Stenograph® CaseCATalyst© software called Brief-It© which opens a window to the right of my transcript screen that makes suggestions for one-stroke codes to replace pounding my machine multiple times for the same phrase. As soon as I implement the new shorter suggestion, it is automatically included in my job dictionary without my having to perform any sort of manual data input procedure. I am certain that companies like Eclipse® and other well-known, time-tested firms who supply machine writers have similar aids.

If you aren't familiar with this great software, call your court reporting program supplier and have them point you in the right direction. Who would say no to producing a transcript with a minimum amount of sweat, stress and strain?

Who's Who in the Law. This is not exactly a technical prep tip, but I think it deserves some print space for those of you ambitious enough to try it.

When I have the opportunity to know ahead of time who the attorneys are going to be for the following day's assignment, I go on the internet and Google both them individually as well as their firms. The result is sometimes a dead end, with only address and telephone number in the offing, but sometimes I hit pay dirt.

The larger law firms are especially good about creating a bio for each of their partners and associates, complete with photos, detailing their education, work history, possible lectures given, and significant cases won. While it's possible another attorney from that firm might show up to pinch-hit in the deposition, chances are you will meet the person you are researching.

Lawyers love to talk (thank goodness), and they particularly love to talk about themselves. What an impression you'd make, greeting an attorney you have never met before by name based on the photo you saw; and how pleasantly unsettling for them if you were to say, "That wrongful death case involving the boat engine exploding, how did you manage to gather all the evidence if the boat sank?"

This needs to be way down on the list of possible things to do to prepare for a deposition, but I have found that interaction with both your clients and other barristers in the room means that you will come to mind that much more when future depositions are set up through that attorney. Besides the more relaxed atmosphere that you create for yourself and others as a result of knowing who you are dealing with in a case, it never hurts to let the attorneys know that you are interested in learning more about litigation per se.

The over-arching purpose here, of course, is to be the creator of a verbatim transcript *and* to enjoy what you are doing to the greatest extent possible!

2
Set the Stage for Success

Many freelance court reporters as well as court reporting agency owners will tell you that arriving 30 minutes in advance of the proceeding start time is sufficient. I like to get there 45 minutes to an hour ahead of time, sometimes to the surprised receptionist's greeting of, "You know the deposition is scheduled for 10 o'clock, not 9 o'clock?"

I don't have a phobia about being late (although the few times that I spent 20 minutes lost driving to the attorney's office, gave me a much-needed time buffer that allowed me to still arrive before the scheduled start). I prefer to be completely set up and in charge of my surroundings before anyone else arrives.

I have a routine that I follow, not necessarily in order, but it serves me well in being completely prepared when the parties enter the room. Create a setup pattern of your own and practice it at home a few times before going on your first job so that you are comfortable with your routine from the get-go.

Setting up. I set up my computer and steno equipment and turn both on. I like to work off the electric rather than the batteries, so I look for the nearest outlet. I like to position myself at the far end of a conference room so that anyone entering will not be greeted by a bunch of wires on the floor. If the only socket available causes my wires to cut across possible foot traffic, I have a roll of gaffer's tape to cover them. Gaffer's tape is superior to other kinds of tape because it doesn't leave any sticky residue on what could be some very expensive carpets.

The exception to setting up at the far end of a conference table is when you are covering a videotaped deposition. In most cases, the videographer positions their equipment at one of the narrow ends of the table and shoots the long way across to the witness sitting at the other end, which is where I normally sit. In that case, you should get comfy on either side of the table as close to the witness as possible. So you will be

12

sitting on the long end of the rectangle, on the same side as the attorney. Show both the videographer and the lawyer next to you consideration, and be sure to ask them if your computer obstructs their line of sight. There are a few things to be aware of in videotaped depositions that don't occur in others, and we will discuss that at the end of this chapter.

Getting the juice. Sometimes I wonder whether anyone took the time to plan the layout of a particular conference room with the needs of today's business people in mind, when the only accessible electric socket is located on the wall in the middle of the room. No problem! I have my trusty extension cord. Between that and a few pieces of well-placed tape to keep the cord out of the way, I am still on top of things.

Writing up your info. With my equipment set up and my carriers neatly tucked in a corner, I am ready to tackle the assignment information input. I have printed out the detail sheets that were emailed to me by my agency.
I now open my DepoBook©, a wonderful product created by the company of the same

name, and start to enter whatever specifics I have. Each two-page section features ample space to put date and time; name and venue of the case; witness names; whether the depo has video; whether the parties order rush delivery, rough copy, realtime; space for a seating chart; and shortcuts that I make up for names and terms that will come up, if I have them.

The best feature of all is the area for business cards. Every time an attorney hands me his card, I have an adhesive area where I stick that card, fill in his case affiliation, and I never, ever have to hunt for that card again. This aid comes in two sizes, one that holds four business cards per page in its sticky grasp, and one that holds as many as eight. Take a look at the sample case information on pages 16 and 17 .

Buy the small one for now, if you are so inclined, as it is more likely as a newbie you will be reporting two-party cases. The multiple-party cases will probably not fall into your hands for a few years, but in case you luck out, you can always use the attorney page blanks left on the page for your previous day's case, and then order some large books for the future!

Establishing the case. Now that your software is up and running, it's time to set up your case for the day. Since there are a number of different software packages both for machine and voice writers, I will address this section generically. Create your file name and designations for each attorney about whom you have information.   If a different attorney happens to show up (see the section on business cards), you can go back into your designations and quickly change them.

The key here is to have as much preliminary setup work done as possible. Look at the parties in the case style, and create short forms or brief codes for them. If Susie Johnson is the plaintiff and Blackwell Motors is the defendant, I will enter those names in my job dictionary as well as create a one-stroke code for Ms. Johnson, for the full name Susie Johnson, for Blackwell, and for Blackwell Motors.

Sometimes we are lucky enough to have a caring secretary escort us to the conference room and ask, "Is there anything you need, water, coffee...?" In that case, it doesn't hurt to ask if it would be possible for him or her to bring in a copy of the pleading or case interrogatories.

○ Original & 1　○ Copy
○ ASCII　○ Amicus
○ Condensed　○ Key Word
○ Rough copy　○ Rough disk

Appearing for: Δ / π /____

○ Paid $_____

Notes:

_____

EMAIL:

KISH & LIETZ, P.C.

PAUL S. KISH
ATTORNEY AT LAW

225 PEACHTREE STREET, N.E.
1700 SOUTH TOWER
ATLANTA, GEORGIA 30303

(404) 588-3991
DIRECT: (404) 588-3992
FAX: (404) 588-3995
E-MAIL: PAUL@LAW-KL.COM

☑ Original & 1　○ Copy
☑ ASCII　○ Amicus
☑ Condensed　☑ Key Word
○ Rough copy　○ Rough disk

Appearing for: Δ ⓟ / **Pltf**

○ Paid $_____

Notes: **Wants exhibits tabbed**

EMAIL: **Deliver by 1/14/11**

O'NEAL, BROWN & GAUTREAUX
A PROFESSIONAL CORPORATION

MANLEY F. BROWN
ATTORNEY AT LAW

SUITE 1001
AMERICAN FEDERAL BUILDING
544 MULBERRY STREET
MACON, GEORGIA 31201-2774
(478) 742-8981
(478) 743-5033 FAX

Email: brown@obglawfirm.com

○ Original & 1　☑ Copy
○ ASCII　○ Amicus
☑ Condensed　○ Key Word
○ Rough copy　☑ Rough disk

Appearing for: ⓓ / π / **Deft**

○ Paid $_____

Notes: **Rough by 9 a.m. tomorrow**

EMAIL:

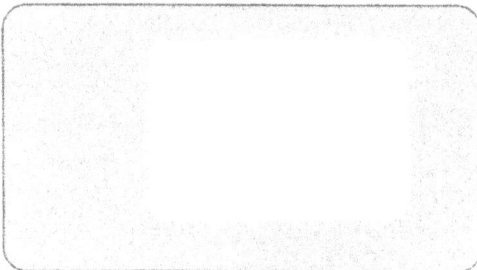

○ Original & 1　○ Copy
○ ASCII　○ Amicus
○ Condensed　○ Key Word
○ Rough copy　○ Rough disk

Appearing for: Δ / π /____

○ Paid $_____

Notes:

_____

EMAIL:

Mileage **140 tot.** Expenses **Tolls $7** Reported for **Kish**

TIME: **10:00 a.m. - 4:05 p.m.** DATE: **1/10/11** S M T W Th F S

SET BY: **Kish**   TAKEN AT: **14 Town Place, Macon, GA**

TRIAL DATE: _____ FILE NAME: **6082** JOB # **1405** JOB DUE: **1/24**

TIME **10:00 - 11:30**
Deponent #1: **Jane Doe**   (**41 pages**)

Address: **85 Seminole Dr., Perry, GA 30253**

TIME **12:45 - 4:05**
Deponent #2: **John Roe**   (**102 pages**)

Address: **18 Barwick Rd., Lynn, GA 30233**

✓VIDEO REAL-TIME INTERPRETER COURT DAY HEARING Statement (✓ Expedite) Hold job **JOB DONE** X

COURT: **State** COUNTY: **Bibb** CASE # **2011-CA-850**

Blackwood Resources, Inc.,

                    Plaintiff,

          vs.

Timothy Harkness,

                    Defendant.

C A S E N A M E

wit
SEATING
me
Brown   Kish
video

EXHIBITS: Δ (π) **1-7 (tabbed for Kish)**

Also present:
Timothy Harkness

Robert Sparks, video

SPELLINGS

Dr. Spears
Dr. Aimes
PW-R = Blackwood Resources
PHR-BG = Mr. Harkness

(witnesses will read)

#Pages **143**
Volume# **1**

In the case of an arbitration, you would ask for the statement of claim.

Those are documents where the whole reason for the lawsuit is spelled out, and there is an absolute treasure trove of names and phrases that will allow you to get familiar with the case quickly, and you will be able to input more information into your glossary even before the words come out of anybody's mouth.

Reassure the secretary that making a copy of the docs for you is not necessary, that you just want to write the info down in your record. Years ago I was able to obtain a statement of claim that dealt with DRIPs, later pronounced by the parties as "drips." I found out, by skimming through the claim document, that this was a technical acronym for direct-reduced iron ore pellets, and the parties were impressed that I was familiar with the term from the start. Little did they know!

A handheld document scanner is a great little gadget that eliminates the need for you asking for copies of papers that might be used during a deposition, but that are not marked as exhibits. In many states, the practice is to give the reporter the marked exhibits at the close of the deposition. You submit them to your agency to be copied and attached to the original transcript.

I don't recommend that you buy a scanner right off the bat when you start your career, but it is a great "toy" to consider when you have some extra funds lying around to invest in your professional comfort (and it's another one of those wonderful, legitimate tax deductions – see Chapter 12).

Premarking exhibits. Some agencies like to provide you with exhibit stickers sporting their company name, and some just provide you with generic stickers.

Exhibits are marked according to the party taking the deposition. If the attorney who hired you represents the defendant, then use stickers that say Defendant's Exhibit. If the plaintiff's firm is the one that is paying for the original transcript, use Plaintiff's Exhibit stickers.

If you have a copy of a notice, which is a document that one side sends to the other side(s) notifying them of the deposition, you will see the attorneys listed and whom they represent. That will let you know whether your client is batting for the plaintiff or defendant. There is always a time when you won't have much information, and in that case, pull out your sheet of generic stickers that just say Exhibit on them and you'll be covered.

Now that you have the correct sheet of stickers in front of you, write the witness' last name in the blank space provided on each of ten stickers, making sure that you have enough room to fit two lines of text in this small space. Next to the witness' last name, number the exhibit sticker starting with 1, put 2 on the next sticker, and so on. In the space you have left under the witness' last name, put your initials in the lower left corner. Next to that, put the date.

It will look something like this:

PLAINTIFF'S EXHIBIT	EXHIBIT	DEFENDANT'S EXHIBIT
Tate 1	Tate	Tate 1
	Claimant 1	
MB 1/12/11	MB 1/12/11	MB 1/12/11

Even if your client later comes in and informs you that they are continuing exhibit numbering from previous depositions, all you will have lost is a few minutes' writing time. What you will have gained is their appreciation that you have the clerical issues under control and you are fully prepared to go forward. Having to stop 30 seconds each time you need to mark a document as an exhibit as opposed to the three seconds it takes to slap a premarked sticker onto the paper will save you and the attorney time. Creating win-win scenarios like this, even in small ways, will go far in building a client following.

Just FYI, if your agency does not provide exhibit stickers for you, there are generic stickers included in the back of every DepoBook©. If you find you are running low on labels after a week or two, there are some solid, reliable companies that have a wide variety to choose from, such as Pengad®, RPM®, and Stenograph®.

The court reporting agency office people responsible for assigning you future jobs will love the fact that, when you turn in your exhibits for copying and attachment to the finished transcript, every exhibit has a label which uniquely identifies it. If an exhibit of yours falls on the production room floor, any employee in that department will be able to return it to its rightful pile based on the information you provided. Making things easy for the support personnel in your agency really pays off and creates a good reputation with everyone connected with converting the spoken word into a certified verbatim transcript.

Business card exchange. Even though you might have already gotten a goodly amount of information about the attorneys who will be participants in your deposition, there is always the possibility that another member of the law firm will substitute in that day. Sometimes more than one attorney in a firm is listed as working on that case.

Now that you are settled in and ready to greet the parties as they arrive, it is good policy to ask for business cards and to give each attorney one of yours. I want to emphasize the word *each*, because there may even be two or more lawyers from the same firm attending. It is good policy not to pass over the junior representatives of a law firm, as they, the paralegals or the secretaries are often the ones hiring the court reporter for future depositions. If a lawyer has your business card, he or she can request you by name. Even if you have no seniority at a freelance agency, a request by a client trumps the choice to use even the most tenured of reporters, and you will get the job.

If the attorney just gave his last card away

and comes to the depo empty-handed, just go with the flow. When asking his or her name, ask if they are associated with the firm listed on the notice, if you have one. "Mr. Smith, are you from Costa Burger?" Since you saw that Costa Burger is reflected on the info you got, you are showing them you have at least a smidgin, if not more, of familiarity with the parties, Even if you are wrong, they will happily correct you. If you are flying blind with no information about the firms, then the question becomes, "Mr. Smith, are you in your own office or are you affiliated with a firm?"

With that info entered into your daybook, be sure to ask for the full mailing address, including zip code, telephone number, fax number, and email address. Many court reporting agencies require that all this data be entered on the appearance page for each firm. It helps in getting the transcript to the right places, and also helps you if you need to call a paralegal with a question.

Make the most of your time. In most cases, when you announce to the receptionist that you are the court reporter with Attorney So-And-So, you will be ushered directly into the conference room where the proceeding will take place. We have already gone over setting up procedures, so at this point we will assume that you are alone, completely prepared, and ready to go when the parties enter.

Before that occurs, assuming you have gotten to the assignment with a very comfortable time buffer of at least 30 to 45 minutes before the scheduled start, it is now time to make your minutes work for you.

Rather than skimming the latest issue of *People Magazine* or surfing the net while you are waiting, open up a file from a job that you have not yet finished and submitted to your agency or your client for production and payment. If you need to listen to your audio, use earphones that you can plug into your computer to ensure privacy both for yourself and for adjacent offices where the walls may be thin.

Queue up the file for today's job, minimize it on the computer, and go to the file you wish to edit from a previous day; or if your software allows, set up today's file and open the previous day's job, being able to toggle right back to today's setup as soon as the deposition is about to start. Our business is often a hurry-up-and-wait sort of deal, where the assigned start time is not always when the job begins (kind of like a commercial airline schedule).

Find out what your agency's policy is as to waiting time. There are some court reporting companies that charge their clients for the reporter being present at the assignment and not writing anything. If you are asked to appear at a deposition that is scheduled for a 10:00 a.m. start and the proceedings are delayed until 10:30 a.m., some agencies allow you to bill for a half hour of waiting time.

Sometimes the parties are close to settlement, and the reporter is asked to remain there until a settlement statement is put on the record, or if the negotiations break down and they decide to go ahead with the examination. In an instance like that, you could be sitting around for a few hours before the lawyers release you. Your time is worth something, especially based on the theory that had you and your agency known that you would not start recording until 2:00 p.m., you might have been able to score a morning assignment.

Be that as it may, you are now stuck waiting, waiting, waiting. Fortunately, you can make this circumstance work for you, and by the time the parties go on the record, you have knocked out a nice portion of your transcription backlog *and* gotten paid the additional waiting time fee! Best of all, you have less work to do when you get home. I call that a win-win-win.

Brown bag it. I like to carry my lunch and a few protein bars with me so that on an all-day assignment I don't waste time and funds going out for lunch. For the most part, luncheon recesses are around an hour, and getting in an extra half hour of transcription at that time as well means less time telling the kids at home that I have to finish my work now, or making the choice to spend evening time with the kids and then staying up into the wee hours of the night to deliver my transcript timely.

Be prepared to spend many hours at the beginning of your career, becoming accustomed to the processes of taking down, transcribing, and proofing your work. You will be pulling down an ample salary in the not-too-distant future, but right now those big bucks seem far-off and almost unattainable.

I guarantee that by the end of your first twelve months as a diligent, disciplined court reporter, you will be familiar enough with the routines and sought after by schedulers that you will be making a very comfortable living and spending half the time working that you do now, producing the very same volume of pages.

If you can deliver 200 pages a week now, working as a diligent newbie, next year you will be sitting on top of 400 pages or more each week. You will have carved out the beginnings of a reputation for yourself in terms of dependability and timeliness; you will have several agencies clamoring for your talents, or one agency whose scheduling department assigns you multi-copy work with the utmost confidence. The underlying principle here is that you want to produce your work such that your professional time is spent in the most efficient way, and your per-hour worth is always climbing.

Call in. At the conclusion of the proceeding, give your agency a call. Let them know you have finished, estimate approximately how many pages you have written according to the computer file indication, or just quote about thirty-five pages per hour and go with that number. While not every reporting company keeps track of those statistics, some schedulers or office managers like to be aware of your backlog or accumulated pages to determine how much more work to give you without overloading you.

Whether they use backlog information or not, rendering this courtesy to an agency tells them you are accustomed to *having* a backlog! Otherwise, how would you even be aware of the necessity to utilize this practice?

Calling in serves another even more vital purpose for your reporting agency in certain circumstances, and that is when you are either directly told or you overhear the attorneys talking about plans for future depositions in the case. In the first instance, one lawyer says to the other something along the lines of, "See you on the 7th for Dr. Roland's deposition." Here's where your little antennae go up, signaling another win-win situation.

Your choices to act in this scenario are many. If the person who makes this comment is your client, you can simply say, "Just to make sure we have that depo on our book, let me confirm that Dr. Roland is on the 7th. And at what time?" Once you have the answer, which could conceivably be a time, or a response of, "We don't know what time yet," you declare, "We may already have it scheduled, but I will make sure our office knows, and we will confirm with your secretary the day before."

If the attorney who talks about Dr. Roland's future appearance in the case is not your client, or if you are not sure who will be the questioner in the future depo, just address the other legal eagles in the room by saying, "Do you have a court reporter that you regularly use, or would you like our service to cover Dr. Roland's examination?" In more than 50 percent of cases, the attorney will have their own reporting company that they utilize. But even so, if you have worked diligently that day, accommodated them with some efficiently delivered readback, there is a good chance that the non-client will say, "Well, since you're already familiar with the case, you might as well report my witnesses too."

Ding Ding Ding! The Daily Double! Now that you are the owner of this marvelous new information, you not only call your agency with an assignment they would not have had on their book if not for you, but you get to declare that you have been *requested* to return on the case. You now have a job scheduled days in advance that, barring an unexpected cancellation, belongs to you. An agency's first mandate is to please the client. Even though you may not have as much experience in the field as some of the other reporters, an attorney's preference for a particular reporter overrides any seniority standing.

You will also be walking into that next deposition with your own research already done: you are familiar with the parties, the spellings of a good number of names, abbreviations for terms that will likely come up, and less time spent during the next session settling into a comfortable cadence, which ordinarily takes a good hour, once you are on the record, in my experience.

Now, not every continuation of a case means that you will garner a request that you return. You still come across to your office, however, as someone who is taking care of business, literally. You are helping your agency keep a happy client (and potentially a new happy client, if the new depo is taken by the other side). The lawyer's secretary and/or paralegal will be delighted that your agency is taking one more chore off of his or her plate by assisting in case management.

Developing these behaviors into habits can only yield favorable outcomes for you. If the non-client attorney does use his own reporter, you have still demonstrated a concern to your client that things run smoothly in the case.

If you are not specifically asked to come back but the client has another witness scheduled, your agency will be grateful for your efficiency, even if the office already has the deposition on their book.

The principle that you are communicating is professionalism beyond your weeks or months of experience. They know that they can depend on you for acting affirmatively on the client's behalf. And they will definitely remember that for future assignments.

3
Swearing in the Witness

This is a simple one, almost a no-brainer. You turn to the witness, ask her to raise her right hand, and administer the oath. Well, it used to be a no-brainer.

It is important to realize that our great country is diverse in so many ways, including religions. Within those religions are groups of believers who are more literal about the concept of swearing, and you may come across someone who says to you, "I will not swear." What do you do?

It is best to administer an oath that acknowledges those beliefs without sacrificing the sanctity and gravamen of the legal promise you are requiring the witness to make. I ask the witness to raise her right hand (and sometimes they prefer not to – that's okay), and I say, "Do you solemnly swear or affirm that the testimony you are about to give will be the truth, the whole truth, and nothing but the truth?" Then all bases are pretty well covered, and their testimony is legally subject to the penalties of perjury if they lie.

Just a quick aside: this does belong in the War Stories chapter, but it is such a quick story, I'll just throw it in here. I did not know that the witness sitting in front of me had had a stroke some months before, and his right hand and arm were unusable. I had not noticed this when he came in because he had placed his right upper extremity (a medical term for the right arm you will hear a lot) in his coat pocket. There appeared to be nothing out of the ordinary regarding that appendage, at least not to me.

When I asked him to raise his right hand, he smiled and told me it didn't work, but he would be happy to raise his *other* right! I was very apologetic, and grateful for his humor in a rare and potentially sticky situation.

Adios, amigo – interpreter depos. A deposition notice that indicates that a foreign language interpreter is required should garner a sigh of relief from the new court reporter. This is an opportunity to create a transcript from slow-moving dialog, being able to put in all the punctuation in the right places right on the job, and breezing through proofreading later on.

A more experienced reporter might find it a bit tedious, as the slower the proceeding, the longer it takes to fill up a transcript with testimony. The interpreter is usually state-licensed, and schooled in the sometimes awkward process necessary to translate legal proceedings.

First, the swearing-in process is a bit different from the norm. Before you swear the witness, you must swear the interpreter. The oath I always administer is as follows: "Do you solemnly swear or affirm that you will faithfully interpret these proceedings from (foreign language) to English and vice versa to the best of your ability?"

After the interpreter answers in the affirmative, you say to her, "Please help me swear in the witness." Then you look at the witness and use the same oath as you would for an English-speaking person. The interpreter will do the translation for everything from there on out.

In your transcript, the first line in your testimony portion will read:

JOAN RIVERA, Interpreter, was duly sworn. Then,

MARIA GOMEZ, called as a witness, having been duly sworn through the interpreter, testified as follows:

The words may be a little different depending on the style required by your agency (see Chapter 7 on the form book), but the concept is the same.

I always add an extra parenthetical in an interpreter-attended deposition right under the witness' swearing that says:

(All questions and answers, except as otherwise indicated, are through the interpreter.)

The reason for that is, the witness may have some understanding of English, and although her attorney may have instructed her to speak only in her native tongue and allow the interpreter to translate, she may go ahead and answer in English without the aid of the translator. In that case, I include a short parenthetical that indicates the answer is in English but directly out of the witness' mouth:

A   (Without the interpreter) I no go to the store. I stay by home.

I use the doubled-up steno stroke **WOUT/WOUT** to tell my computer to set up the A and the parenthetical without my having to pound on the keys too much. This way, my transcript is completely true to what is occurring during the proceedings.

A note of caution, for your sake and the sake of the transcript: Do NOT tolerate an interpreter speaking in the third person when translating. Occasionally you will run into an inexperienced person whose training is not strictly litigation-oriented, and that person will translate an answer by saying, "She said (meaning the witness said) she went to the store." It is the legal interpreter's mandate to translate in the first person. That answer should be, "I went to the store." The translation is always to be spoken by the interpreter as if the witness herself is speaking.

If you find yourself in this predicament, simply turn to the interpreter, risk interrupting the questioning attorney (who is sometimes clueless about this procedure), and instruct the translator: "Excuse me, Ms. Interpreter, but please translate the answers in the first person." It may take a few times to get the translator back on the right track, and you won't win any popularity contests with her, but it will save you from having to certify a transcript that will be judged second-rate.

4
What Do Attorneys Think About Us?

There are a number of ways to get feedback that lead to us showing up as the consummate reporting professionals, both in the act of reporting proceedings as well as in our approach to transcription and ultimate delivery of the product. I have taken what could be termed a straw poll among a wonderful cross-section of the legal litigation field. This chapter demonstrates some of what NOT to do on an assignment. It doesn't matter whether the attorneys are accurately recounting their observations or not; this can serve to shine a spotlight on the potential assumptions our clients can make based on our behavior.

Interrupting. There are just times when the witness or the lawyer picks up a document and starts reading from it like their hair is on fire. If you want to get a verbatim record, you have to interrupt. "Excuse me, counsel. Could you please read a little slower?"

Sometimes the witness and the lawyer talk over each other in a verbal jousting that makes me want to grind my teeth. I put up one hand as if to say, "Hey, guys, my fingers are not on the keys, you need to pay attention to this." I quickly say in a loud, firm voice, "I can't take the both of you at the same time."

There are also times when I just hunker down and report the words as best I can, with plans of filling the transcript later with dashes to show how each person is cutting the other off. During the first break, I quietly go over to the questioning attorney and tell him he HAS to let the witness finish, or his transcript will look choppy.

Since your deposition is often the first time the witness has testified in any sort of legal proceeding, I feel it is the attorneys' purview to keep the record clean. So if the witness is the primary offending party, I ask the lawyer who is representing him to tell his client to please wait until the questioner is finished before talking.

You did *what?* The bad news is that people

do not change their speaking habits the instant that you make a request of them to do so. After I have brought up the situation, I hunker down and create the transcript that the parties are allowing me to create. Sometimes it isn't pretty. But it is pretty accurate.

One attorney was very surprised when a court reporter put her hand up to silence the witness, then said, "Hang on. I got to catch up." She typed a little more, then she said, "Okay, go on."

According to the lawyer's story, she did this throughout the deposition, even interrupting in the same fashion two or more times during a single answer! The attorney was angry, convinced that the reporter was not fast enough, and commented that chopping up the testimony as it was being given made for a disjointed interrogation that threw everyone off all day.

While there are three sides to every story like this, the lawyer's, the reporter's, and the truth, it points up the delicate balance you need to maintain between inserting yourself unnecessarily into the proceedings and protecting the record. Bottom line, you have to use your intuition when to take a stand for your sanity. A deposition with heated interruption going on all day will take its toll on you. Simply inform the parties of the difficulty you are having at the first break, and perform your duties knowing that they are on notice that the transcript might very well look like crap:

Q   *When did you think the –*
A   *I'm not sure.*
Q   *-- police officer got mad and –*
A   *I'm not sure.*
Q   *-- wrote a ticket? You said you're --*
A   *Not sure. Can I –*
Q   *Go ahead.*
A   *-- just say something?*

Just writing this out as an example for you makes me shudder. It does happen from time to time, and you need to be prepared. As time passes and you gain experience working in this field, you will have a better sense of when to interrupt and when to keep silent and bear down.

An important component to making this decision easier is to continue to practice after you graduate school, to attain even higher levels of competency (see Chapter 5). That way, even when the motormouths decide that they want to hold their convention in your jurisdiction, you have it all covered!

Asking for spellings. Just like in the section above, the song that attorneys sing is that the flow of Q and A is broken when the court reporter interrupts. The harmony that we add is, sometimes it is essential to interrupt when the proceeding is spinning out of control, and we have to cause a break in the flow in order to regain that control.

When someone mentions a name or term that you have never heard before, do not stop the testimony to have someone spell it for you. Save your interruption cards for when you really need them. In the meanwhile, write (steno) or dictate (voice) the name phonetically until the first break.

Writing the words you need spellings for on a pad you keep close by will make it a simple task to get the information at the next recess. If questions and answers are flying back and forth at a rapid pace and you don't have the time to put pen to paper, don't worry.

Create an arbitrary code that you can put in right at the time the mystery word is uttered, and at a break you can go back through the file and scan (I use **KH-BG**), looking for that specific code. Then you can write the words on your pad and get spellings before the break is over.

Don't be intimidated by the parties coming back into the room and wanting to get started after *their* break is done. You have been working through the recess to clarify names and terms you were not given beforehand (sometimes questioners will ask for the spelling from a witness right during the testimony, but that is not the norm). Simply say, "Before we begin, I'd like to take a minute to get the correct spelling," and then pronounce each name you have listed.

When you assume... Let me take a moment here to point out that it is very important not to assume the common spelling for a name. Just because Mr. "Smith" was the person that the witness spoke to, don't leave the deposition at the end of the day believing that it's okay to simply plug in what you think is the most likely way to spell "Smith." Smyth, Smitt; there could be a few variations.

Some years back, a gentleman entered the conference room and introduced himself to me as "Joseph Clark." Since this was a last-minute assignment, the only information I was given about the case was the address, my client's name, and the time it would start (see Chapter # about call-ons). I politely asked him if he spelled his name with an E or without an E. He politely replied, "With an E."

The witness was sworn, and the attorney began her questioning:

Q   Can you please state your name and spell it for the record?

A   Josef, J-O-S-E-F, Kloarque, K-L-O-A-R-Q-U-E.

The man's family had come from the Netherlands generations ago, so he was an American citizen without a hint of a foreign accent. That was a great lesson for me. Now when a name comes up that I want to make an assumption about, I still ask for the spelling, but save the possibly common names for the end, saying, "And Jones and Martin, those are the common spellings, J-O-N-E-S and M-A-R-T-I-N?" That way if the person giving you the information thinks the common spellings of Joehnz and Maertyn are different than yours, you've got it covered.

Keeping interruptions to a minimum, yet maintaining the accuracy and integrity of your transcript will go far in establishing your reputation as the consummate reporting professional. I have often laughed when an attorney has complimented me on a good job after a deposition has concluded based on the fact that I did not interrupt. It almost begs the question of, *how do you know? You haven't seen the transcript yet!* But combining the knowledge of when to interrupt and when not to, with the speed and accuracy that you garner in school and reporter study groups, will earn you the highest praises and the best assignments.

Certifying the question. There are times when a witness refuses to answer the question posed based on the recommendation of his attorney. If the questioner wants to persuade the judge at a later time to instruct the witness to answer, your client may say, matter-of-factly, "Certify that question."

The first time I heard that, I was at a loss. I didn't know what official duty I was to perform at that juncture. I had a vision of taking out a giant foam-rubber mallet and banging my steno machine with it, like a judge sounding his gavel. Thankfully, it is much simpler than that.

There is no formal certification per se that

we as reporters confer on a particular question. As a courtesy to the attorneys, what we are to do is create a section just at the end of the exhibit page (this positioning has been my experience; check with your agency to make sure this is where they want it).

The section is entitled Certified Questions. Underneath that you will have two columns, one labeled Page and the other labeled Line. You merely note the page and line numbers of the questions that were requested to be certified. You only need to put the page number and line number of the location of where the question starts. And that's all there is to it. So when, "Certify that question," is uttered, you can now simply indicate with a slight nod of the head that you understand the direction!

Timing is everything. It is inexcusable to be late. It is inexcusable to be late. Did I say it is inexcusable to be late?

Of course, there are those incidences where there is an unavoidable delay, an emergency of some sort. But scheduling your trip to a deposition so that you will arrive 15 minutes ahead of time does not work. The possibility of running into a snag that will make you late is too great.

Attorneys may accept your apology as you rush to set up your equipment, but they are not happy. At three to four hundred dollars an hour collectively for the billing time of just two associate attorneys working a case (the hierarchy is senior partner, partner, associate), a delay of even a quarter hour can cost their clients plenty; not to mention the time of a physician witness who could be charging six hundred or more an hour to the attorney who hired you.

If you are afflicted with terminal tardiness or chronic skin-of-your-teeth arrival syndrome, the cure is a very simple one. Imagine that waiting for you at the door of your deposition destination is a business envelope. In it is a cashier's check for one million dollars. The only condition for keeping the money is that you arrive no later than 45 minutes ahead of the scheduled proceeding time. Guaranteed, that million will ensure the lateness factor being reduced to a fraction of a fraction.

There are some circumstances where lateness to a job can not be avoided. When the assigned reporter is ill and a replacement has to be found instantly to cover the depo, I have gotten a frantic call from my office: "Fran can't make it to her job. It's in an hour. You're the closest one to the address. Can you take it?"

Based on the facts that the examination is taking place at a company that is 40 minutes from my house; that, having taken the day off to transcribe at home, I am in my jammies; and I have no information about the case save my client's name, the hosting attorney's name, and an abbreviated suit name; I ask my office manager to call the attorneys and inform them that I might be late.

I always have a set of work clothes ready to go in case of calls like this, and I have gotten myself together and out the door in less than 10 minutes (see Chapter 6). A word of caution: I refuse to get a speeding ticket, or worse yet, get into an accident because I am rushing to a job. But I am prepared for the possibility that there will be a few unhappy faces when I get to my destination.

Because I pride myself on being punctual, I am very uncomfortable arriving late. The first thing I do when I am ushered into the conference room is apologize for inconveniencing those assembled. I never say, "Well, it was the other reporter who got sick, and

I just got the call." Rocks are hard and water is wet. The reporter representative of my agency (me) is either late or is not late. And I am late.

So I whip out my computer, boot it up while I set up my steno machine, and say, "Ms. Smith?" to confirm she is the client; ask the last name of the opposing attorney; and get the correct spelling of the witness' name. My computer is now ready, and I create a file simply called "Today" and tell the parties I can proceed. It usually takes five to seven minutes from first entering the room to swearing the witness.

At the first break, I will do all the proper setup, record information in my daybook, get business cards, etc. But right now, time is money. It's not a great feeling to be rushed and have people glowering at you because you are the only player not ready to go. So save those experiences for when you are the only hope for your agency to cover their assignment.

And by the way, each time you help them out in this way, you will enhance your by now blossoming reputation.

Wait, wait, don't tell me. From time to time, at the end of a deposition when you are packing up and everyone but your client has left the room (or even at a recess), the attorney will turn to you and say, "You're unbiased. What do you think of the witness? What do you think of the other side's case?"

The tendency is to give your opinion. Don't. After thirty years, there are times when I respond to inquiries like this with comments like, "I can understand the reason for the suit, but it seems that a jury may not be sympathetic to a witness like him," or something that is fairly vague.

You are just at the beginning of your career, and you don't have enough experience to draw on as a reporter to answer from that perspective. As a layperson, you may have great insight, but it is best to keep it to yourself. If the attorney has brought the suit, he already knows the merits, and if you have an opinion contrary to his, you may annoy him. Why take the chance? Go home and share your opinion of the case or the witness with your fellow reporters when you meet to do group practice (see Chapter 5), and stay out of hot water.

The magic of court reporting. One of the things that always surprises me is the attorneys' assumption that if I blend into the wallpaper for the duration of the proceeding, that I am doing a good job. More than once, when I have had no reason to interrupt, read back, or mark exhibits, I have been complimented: "Thanks for your help. You're really good."

At that moment, I can't help but wonder if a monkey dressed in my clothes and seated in that conference room banging at the steno machine would have received the same praise; yet this highlights an important point.

The legal professionals around us in the field, be they lawyers, paralegals, or secretaries, assume that if we are sitting at the head of that table, we are qualified to do so; otherwise we would not have been sent there. At times, a reporter with more experience and familiarity with the content of the case will be unable to cover his or her job at the last minute due to some emergency, and you will be grabbed and sent over to cover that depo. It may not be the most honored way to be given the chance for you to demonstrate to the agency scheduler that you are up to the task, but it gets you another opportunity to show your capabilities.

You may still be a little green around the gills, but the people attending the deposition don't know that. So act like you don't know that either! Every hour spent reporting is experience that will benefit you going forward. And every word you record brings you closer to the time when you will be uploading or delivering a finished transcript.

So in the beginning of your career, if each time you enter a room to perform court reporting duties you feel a bit awkward, kind of like a monkey fooling with a bunch of strange equipment in front of people who know what they're doing, think of this small piece of advice: Stop it! They don't know that you don't know everything there is to know about reporting. Just take a few deep breaths and remind yourself what it took to get you to where you are right now.

And get to work!

5
Practice, Practice, Practice!

Well, how about you! Look at you, all suited up, a real court reporter, poised to make tons of money after having slogged through class after class of training for a profession that most people are totally unaware even exists. I, for one, am enormously proud of you!

Now to give you a little advice going forward that you may not want to hear: you need to continue practicing. Yes, you are an authentic, credentialed court reporter; but in stressful situations, such as a heated argument between attorneys, heart-rending testimony from a distraught witness, or even a psychotically-motivated alien sighting deposition (see Chapter 14 on war stories), you will lose some speed. You may get distracted to the point where your skill set is affected. Not to worry, there are ways over, around, and through this issue. The foundation for the solution is continuing to practice *after* you have begun working.

Many ways to skin a CAT. There is not just one method to practice once you are out there working. Some court reporting schools have night or weekend classes that cater to a 225 wpm-plus student body. Some schools complain that they would set up such a class if there were more interest. Some proactive reporters pull together a weekly speed session, kind of like a support group.

Four or five people meet with their equipment, set up a CD player with five-minute takes in fast-paced Q&A, literary and medical, and then take turns reading back. Not only does that promote speed building, it also allows you to compare notes with other reporters. Contact with like-minded individuals in your profession is vital:

Reporter One: "What if a lawyer asks me to read something back from an hour ago, how do I handle it?"

Reporter Two: "Oh, that happened to me last week. This is what I did."

Reporter Three: "That's good, but I have an

even better way." And so on, and so on.

Set reasonable goals. Jam sessions, as I call them, are great, but are no substitute for practicing at home. Create a practice declaration for yourself, that you are going to practice four days a week for a duration of one hour. Now, understand that circumstances will always arise to sabotage that goal. The lawyer you were in deposition with yesterday called and decided that instead of being satisfied with receiving the transcript in two weeks, she desperately needs the record in her office *tomorrow afternoon.* Your planned rendezvous with the practice group tonight will have to wait.

Be flexible. One group practice session and three additional one-hour home sessions may have to turn into one one-hour session and four half-hour practices spread over the week. The object is to keep those hands moving or that voice speaking at an increasingly faster rate.

All work and no play. You've been working like a crazy person for six months, and you decide to take a week off and relax. Be certain that all your work has been finished and submitted to your agency before leaving. When you return, unpack, change into some comfortable clothes, and set up your equipment. Take at least an hour to practice the day before you go on your first assignment after vacation. You don't want to be warming up in the bullpen while you're already out on the pitcher's mound.

Go west, young reporter! For those who harbor a dream of moving away from wherever you are now, increasing your speed and accuracy can have another benefit. Look to your national organization and review the requirements for the advanced certificates. Plan on taking and passing those tests. While it's just nice to hang the NCRA Certificate of Merit, with its lovely embossing and fancy lettering, on the wall in your home, that achievement speaks volumes to an agency a thousand miles away who is considering hiring you.

That little piece of paper tells them that you have achieved a distinction beyond the standard requirements, and that, coupled with a well-crafted resume including recommendations from your current agency, will make you a prime candidate for hire. Then all that's left is to rent a

U-Haul and head out!

Whether you are happy where you are or have dreams of relocating, whether you are a freelancer or working in court, increasing your speed and accuracy above the basic requirements will support you in your chosen occupation. Who can say no to less stress, less hours, and more pay? And of course the side benefit is increased pride in the professional you are and are becoming.

6
Dress Like You Mean It!

All right, you have graduated court reporting school and you have a certificate or degree in hand; you're ready to jump on any medical, legal, or off-the-wall terminology that hits your ears; and you are writing at the speed of light. What's missing? A job!

Court reporting has its seasonal ups and downs, but in the three-plus decades that I have been in this profession, even during the two recessionary periods in our economy, I have never experienced a prolonged period of down time. In fact, this is a great career to have, as in leaner economic times, more companies tend to avoid paying their bills and honoring their contracts, reasoning that it is better to take a chance at being sued. More lawsuits mean more depositions.

Enter the court reporter!

Intern like a pro. The biggest hurdle for the new court reporter is getting his or her foot in the door of a good agency, one which is willing to give a novice a chance. Many schools have as part of their program a requirement that the senior reporting student shadow both in-court and freelance reporters for as much as 100 hours before attempting to enter the work force. Aside from the obvious learning in a real-life setting that this provides, you have the opportunity to start to develop your professional persona with a representative of an agency that, based on the impression you make with the seasoned reporter you are shadowing, could yield a real job opportunity.

When sitting in, make it a practice of dressing in business attire. While that might seem like a no-brainer, many students make the mistake of assuming that since they are "only" students, they are virtually invisible. They come to an assignment dressed casually. Although the attorneys and even the working reporter may not say anything, believe me, this does not go unnoticed.

Dress for less. Once you're out there working, always dress in a suit, or the equivalent. Since most of you have some pretty hefty loans to pay off, you may cry out indignantly, "I can't afford to go out and spend hundreds of dollars on fancy suits before I even get my first paycheck!" No worries. You may eventually end up trekking over to Nordstrom's for a shopping spree, but for now, you can do very well looking over your wardrobe and adding some basic professional pieces from the clothing departments in Walmart or K-Mart. Just a few basic purchases will give you the classic look you seek without ripping the heart out of your wallet.

I find it an advantage to be a freelance reporter, from the clothing perspective, in that for the most part I am scheduled to be with different clients on different cases every day. If I choose to, I can wear the same suit a few days in a row, just by changing the shirt. Of course, let's not take that too far. We do like to adhere to the maxim that cleanliness is next to achieving 100 percent in a 300 word per minute Q&A take!

The principle here is if you respect yourself, you will command respect from those in your working environment without ever having to open your mouth. I can't count the number of times I have been asked by a receptionist whether I am from the opposing counsel's law firm because she assumed I was on the legal team rather than the court reporter. While I am cognizant of the complexities of practicing law, and acknowledge that I don't have the extensive training it takes to be an attorney, I stand firmly for myself as a vital part of the process that takes place in this arena. And I am determined to look the part.

7
The Job Interview

Getting your foot in the door at a court reporting agency is easier than you might imagine. Sometimes it takes a familiarity with the language they speak to create a connection with the owner or his or her office personnel.

First and foremost, come dressed to the interview as if you are already being sent on an assignment. Show them you are every inch the professional in your "power duds"! Professional attire indicates that you respect the job you want, and you appreciate its importance. And I know you know what I'm talking about; you just read Chapter 6 on appropriate dress!

Show 'em who you are. A great majority of newly graduated court reporters are, shall we say, more mature. You have had other jobs or careers, and this experience, whether or not you enjoyed it at the time, comes in handy when communicating your ability to take care of business in whatever arena you find yourself. Come with a nicely arranged resume in hand, not more than one page long, and have it electronically configured so you can email it at their request. Be sure to indicate on the resume what kind of CAT (computer-aided transcription) software you are on, and at what speed you have been certified as a result of graduation as well as through national certification, if any. When putting in personal references, be sure to include at least one that is related to court reporting. It is more than likely that you have shadowed a senior reporter for in-field hours as a prerequisite to graduating from your court reporting school, so get in touch with one or more of those people and ask them if you can use their name as a reference.

If you get a refusal from a potential reporting reference, don't be discouraged; be honest and forthright. Ask them frankly where they see a need for improvement, and take it seriously. It may not be about you at all, but negative feedback is just as important as positive. Remind yourself that feedback is merely information, and not a criticism of you as a person. After all, you have spent a ton of time focusing on a very difficult training and you are now on the brink of a fabulous career. Someone viewing your demeanor or skill set from a place of experience can only serve to empower you. Besides, there are other references you can use, and these second-stringers may prove to be more significant than your original choice.

Make certain that you follow a business resume template available through many computer programs, at least one of which is probably already loaded on to your computer. Microsoft Word has several models of resume if you simply type in the word "resume" in the "Type a question for help" section.

Be professionally curious. Asking questions during the interview is more important than you might think, if they are the right questions. If you speak in the language of the court reporting agency, the interviewer will connect with those terms and assume that you are familiar with much more than the average novice reporter, such as:

Do you have a form book? A form book is pretty self-explanatory to the seasoned reporter. Many agencies will have preferences in how the transcript is to appear. It is a non-judicial preference, simply an identifying style that they use to create a sort of brand identity with their clients. Some will ask that a box surround the transcript; some want the index (the listing of the marked exhibits, their description, and location in the transcript) placed after the appearance page (the listing of participating attorneys' names and addresses), and some require the index to be the last page after the certificate.

Do you prefer to keep an electronic signature on file? The agency will give you a link that allows you to forward to them a facsimile of your signature. This is not required, but it sure saves a lot of leg work on your part. Once you have emailed your file to the agency, their production department can affix the electronic signature to the certificate page. Not having to go into the agency office to sign your transcripts can save you hours of time, and keeping down the amount of time spent in clerical details is a great way to maximize the value of the hours you put into this job.

What is your turnaround time? I get my regular delivery jobs in within 10 business days or less. The translation may be very obvious: From the time you are reporting the proceedings to the time that you have proofread that transcript and sent it to the agency, no more than two weeks has elapsed. There are some agencies that will pay you a small premium for any work turned in in five business days.

The bottom line for these companies is timely delivery of transcript. There are some reporters who have been in the field for many years who take even three or (heaven forbid) four weeks to produce a transcript. Exhibiting a sensitivity to the time-specific nature of this business will go far in persuading an agency that you are serious and committed.

Do you ever have out of town assignments? I am happy to travel locally, or even farther. This is something firms love to hear, even if they don't have much travel. In the larger metropolitan areas, reporters with greater seniority in a freelance agency often prefer to work within a couple-mile radius of their office. To them, the world is flat, and those who dare to venture beyond the environs of the city will sadly fall over the edge, never to be heard from again. I capitalize on that mindset, and as a result, often get assignments that take me in the opposite direction of rush-hour traffic.

There is the chance that a case where you have to travel more than 50 miles from your agency may result in a lower page count at the end of the day; but I find it worthwhile to have the agency call me to drive an hour south of Atlanta to cover a deposition on a day when there are few assignments in the city. In that case, the scheduler will forget about seniority and call on those who have come through for the office in the past.

A word of caution: Do not declare that you are willing to travel if your personal life can't handle it. Child care issues can get hairy if you are two hours from home at 4:00 p.m., the depo is still going, and the after-care closes at six. Also, be sure to keep your car in good shape. Regular maintenance might not have been as important in the past, but if you opt to travel locally, you are going to pile on the miles.

Do you pay a differential to reporters who are nationally certified at speeds and accuracy above the basic requirements? For machine writers, there are the RPR, the RMR, the CRR, and the RDR (Registered Professional Reporter, Registered Merit Reporter, Certified Realtime Reporter, and Registered Diplomate Reporter, respectively) given by the NCRA. There are similar certificates that can be attained through the NVRA. Additionally,testing relating to CART (Computer-Aided Real Time) and broadcast captioning is also available, but we will not discuss those here, as they don't relate directly to the sort of work I am talking about. Attaining the RMR, CRR, etc. is not only a feather in your cap, but in some cases can mean more dough in your pocket. With some agencies, your additional qualifications warrant merit increases in the page rate.

Is there a differential based on technical difficulty? Some agencies will give you a slightly larger portion of the page rate that they charge to their clients based on the level of technical difficulty the assignment presents. A deposition of a doctor, whether testifying as an expert or testifying as a treating physician, is considered technical. Generally, any witness who will be testifying as an expert in a case brings his or her own set of verbiage that you will likely not hear in any other setting.

Being willing to take down a record that may take longer than a Workman's Compensation or car accident plaintiff is a plus, and will get you not only more work because you are happy to do it (put that smile on your face when you say "yes"), but also because there are plenty of reporters who don't want to stretch and would rather stay home than tackle a challenge.

What is your basic page rate for an 0 plus one, and what is your basic copy rate? I am so used to saying the phrase, "oh plus one" – meaning original transcript and one copy, that it seems like clear, common English to me. But it is professional jargon meaning the basic order of transcript that is delivered to the client attorney. 0 plus 2 ("oh plus two") connotes that the attorney defending the deposition, the one who initially participates by making objections to the form (see the chapter on common legal phrases used during deposition), has ordered a copy as well.

The good news is, in most areas of the country, every time another attorney shows up, appearing on behalf of another party (in medical malpractice suits, for example, a doctor may be represented by one law firm, a hospital by another, et cetera), there is the possibility that the attorney will order a copy of the transcript. In that case, for no more work than you would put into an original plus one transcript order, you will get an additional copy sale. For example, if an original and one copy pays you $2.00 per page, and additional copies are $1.00 per page, you receive $3.00 per page for an 0+2, and $4.00 per page for an 0+3.

There are some parts of the US where the reporter is not paid additional monies for additional copies. The positive tradeoff there is that the basic per-page pay that you receive is higher. Some reporters are more comfortable with that arrangement because they don't concern themselves whether Lawyers A and B both order the transcript, or only Lawyer A orders.

Just as an aside, be sure to ask your prospective agency whether they have paper order forms that they want attorneys to sign. At the conclusion of the deposition, it is customary for you to ask the parties, "Is two weeks (the usual time taken by agencies to produce the transcript) sufficient, or do you need the deposition delivered more quickly?" You may need to have them sign an order form. If the agency does not use order forms, make sure you get the attorneys' orders recorded before you shut your equipment down. Then note in your assignment book that you did record their orders. That will save a lot of aggravation down the road if an unscrupulous attorney decides to claim that he never ordered the transcript (but has had enough time to make a copy of it in his office). A signed order form or simple sound bite emailed off to him is often the quickest and most painless way of settling such disputes.

If the parties decide to hold off ordering the transcript, what is the billing procedure I should follow? There is also the possibility that the parties are close to settlement, so they want to delay the expense of having the proceedings transcribed. There is different terminology used for this instance, but it is often called a hold. Different agencies have varying policies how the reporter is paid, whether on an hourly appearance basis, estimated pages basis (where you bill for 50 percent of the total), or on a flat session hold fee.

For the most part, the bottom line amounts for all three practices are pretty close, but to avoid submitting an invoice to your agency that does not speak their language and that causes a possible delay in proper billing, ask about it in advance of filling out the paperwork.

Do you have an internet repository or portal for me to upload my work, or do you have a particular person that I email the ASCII files to? The ASCII (pronounced "as-key") file is the electronic version of your testimony from which the agency creates the hard transcript, the electronic transcript with all the bells and whistles that paralegals love, and a word index, which is a listing at the back of the transcript of every word uttered in the proceeding and how many times it appears.

The larger agencies have an internet site that is exclusive to their company where you can upload the various components of your file for that case, including the raw notes, the ASCII, and the audio, if available. It is password-protected, and their production personnel receive notification as soon as you click "Upload" that your case is ready to be transformed into a transcript, and your hard work is ready to be transformed into those lovely dollars and cents!

Do you need me to call in when I'm finished with my morning job? This is a great question to ask, because it assumes that you will be getting morning assignments (often preferable to afternoon ones, since the possibility of going past the noon hour and translating into an all-day job is greater than with an afternoon assignment. As the new kid on the block, you should expect to get more afternoon jobs, or those morning jobs that look to be highly likely not to take very long, such as a Workers' Compensation deposition.

Most importantly, this question implies that you are sensitive to the needs of the office personnel, who can receive several call-ons or spot calls in a day (each geographical region has its own label for an assignment filled on the day it is scheduled). You are telling them that you will make yourself available as needed. Refer back to Chapter 2 for more details about this.

Each court reporting company has its own procedures, so once they welcome you aboard, ask how quickly you can be trained to use their uploading tools. They will trip over themselves getting you all the information you request, because even though you may not have a great deal of experience, they will know you are jumping into your profession with both feet.

You have embraced some very unusual training for a very unusual profession, and emerged successfully. Remember how many people who started in your theory class didn't make it? Perseverance, enthusiasm, and a willingness to be open to a challenge is what got you to this point. Continue with the same mindset, and you will do great, and get paid handsomely for it!

8
Smile: You're (Not) on Video!

When you are assigned your first videotaped deposition, don't go out and buy a new outfit just for the occasion. You will not be on camera at any time. In fact, you will be an invisible voice swearing in the witness and possibly reading back during the deposition if requested. That is all of you that the jury may eventually hear if the tape is played to them at trial.

The procedure is just a little different from that which you follow going into a plain old "vanilla" deposition. It will seem a bit strange the first time, but the changes are minimal and easy to get used to.

First, as explained in a previous chapter, you seat yourself differently. In most cases, you are not at the end of the conference table but just to the side of the witness, between him and one of the attorneys, but sharing the side of the table with the attorney, as the witness is going to be facing the video camera full-on.

Sound check. The videographer will mike up the various parties – but not you. He will likely have the same notice or style of the case (Smith v. Jones) that you do, but sometimes he will ask to copy your information. Most videographers, whether in-house at the court reporting agency or hired independently, have equipment to separately yield either a digital or audiocassette recording of the deposition. Tell the video guy you might need a copy of his audio.

This is in no way implying that you should depend on *anyone else* to get your verbatim record, but if you experience some problem with your equipment, or if the witness is very difficult to understand, you will have an additional backup to check your transcript when proofreading.

If you don't mind earphones, a pair of them with a long cord that the videographer can plug directly into his audio feed is a lifesaver when you have a witness who mumbles. I have had instances where I am literally 18 inches from the deponent's mouth and I have trouble hearing him. To keep from interrupting on a video (which is to be avoided), I have gratefully hooked up to the videographer's audio feed and was able to hear every wheeze and sigh.

Action! Back to the normal procedure in a video depo. You've gotten set up on your side of the table, the parties are seated and miked up, and everyone is ready to go. The first thing that happens is the videographer asks if everyone is ready, and then he gives a preliminary speech which you take down. Create a designation in your colloquy dictionary for THE VIDEOGRAPHER as a speaker so you don't have to do it over and over again for each new video job. Remember, it's all about making your professional life easy and fun.
The cameraman then says any variation of, "This is the videotaped deposition of John Smith in Case Number 1000-CV-2001. This is Tape 1. The time is 9:23 a.m. and the date is February 12, 2012. My name is David Ross, I am the videographer, and the court reporter is Maxyne Bursky. Will the parties please state their appearance and affiliation for the record, and the witness will be sworn."
Get ready for a whirlwind of names. The

attorneys will spit out their names, law firms, and who they represent like the devil is chasing them. And before you know it, the announcements have stopped and you are still furiously committing what they have said to your raw transcript. Then there's silence. They are waiting for you to swear in the witness.

Don't be concerned that the tap-tap-tap of your steno keys or the delay in finishing up your dictation is causing a problem or that the parties are thinking that you aren't doing your job. It is expected that you will play catch-up during the identification of the parties. Besides, anything that you drop, you need not worry; you already have their business cards, you have written down whom they represent, and who is in the room. So you have it locked down tight no matter what.

There is no special procedure for swearing in the witness that is different from a non-videoed deposition, so ask him to raise his right hand, and off you go.

Give me a break. Recesses and off-the-record discussions are formally announced in a video deposition. When Attorney One says, "This is a good time to take a few minutes," don't stop recording the proceedings yet. It is still the videographer's duty is to then say a variation of, "Going off the video record at 11:23 a.m," (which you take down). Then you can get your much-deserved break.

Like wise, when going back on the record, the videographer will instruct the attorneys to stand by, then announce (which you take down), "We are back on the record at 11:34 a.m." He may also indicate that the deposition is now being videoed on Tape 2, and so on.

At the end of the examination, when the last attorney says to the witness, "That's it. Thank you, Mr. Smith, for coming," do not go off the record until you have recorded the videographer's statement of, "This is the end of Tape 3 in the deposition of John Smith. The time is now 4:23 p.m."

Then you pack up, get the videographer's copy of the audio if you need it, and head for the door. It's time to pat yourself on the back for another job well done.

9
Readback: Don't Worry, Be Happy

You have spent years perfecting your craft in school. Countless hours have been devoted to increasing your speed to the point where you can take on any verbal racer who dares to enter your territory. But there is a nagging little voice in the back of your head that whispers, "What if they ask me to read back and I don't have it?"

In spite of the fabulous training you have received, and the devotion you have dedicated to court reporting, the reality is that there may very well come a time where circumstances result in your having missed a word or phrase in a question or answer, and the next sound you hear is, "Would you please read that back?"

The hair on the back of your neck begins to rise; you have a sick feeling in the pit of your stomach. You turn to your computer screen or machine readout and, mustering all the calm and professionalism you can, read back what you have, waiting for the Sword of Damocles to swing down and chop you into little pieces. The attorney may say, "That question was garbled. Let me ask it again." The witness may say, "That's not what I said," and her lawyer may say, "Repeat your answer."

It is unlikely that you will mess up on your readback. More unlikely still will an attorney openly criticize you if you were to stumble or omit a word when reading back.

While your mandate is to be verbatim, there are a few editorial actions, as it were, that you can be aware of to ensure that your readback will be flawless in even the most trying circumstances. This is a bit controversial, as it involves purposefully dropping words, so I encourage you, as I did in the introduction, to determine whether this procedure is right for you. There are purists among veteran court reporters who would not brook the suggestion I am about to make, and there are also those who will nod knowingly, having been there and done that. Only you can decide whether this will serve you in the course of your takedown.

There are times when you walk into a case

and the attorneys are verbally at each other's throats. As soon as the question is asked, an objection flies from the defender's mouth, catching or over-talking the end of the questioner's words. You are working very hard to keep the transcript looking clear as you furiously focus on keeping up.

Suddenly, after the objection, the interrogating lawyer counters his opponent, demanding to know why an objection was made to a perfectly good inquiry. The objecting attorney fires back a response, and the bickering is off and running for what seems like an eternity, even though it could very well last less than a minute. Then come the dreaded words, "We've been arguing so much, I forgot the question." And you silently invoke the power of a higher being, praying that you have the offending question in its entirety.

Don't panic. A way that I utilize to ensure that my readback is perfect under these circumstances is to focus intently on recording the entire question, throwing down a cursory stroke indicating the opposing attorney is objecting. By that time, it is likely that I have missed some of the colloquy because I was busy getting the full question into my transcript.

The likelihood that counsel will request I read back their objections and argument is as certain as my winning the lottery. The likelihood that counsel will ask me to read back the question is as certain as my tearing up worthless lottery tickets every week. I'll take Door Number Two.

In a working situation where the speed of attorney-to-attorney interaction is pushing the envelope of your abilities, of primary importance is preserving the testimony. Of course, every word uttered is vital, but this is a way to work through an emergency circumstance and come out the other side in one piece.

When I have emerged from a particularly difficult assignment, I will make time over that very week to spend a few hours practicing with speed tapes. There is always a challenge out there in one way or another, and it is essential that you meet it accountably. See my chapter on practicing. After more than three decades of court reporting, improving my technical skills is still part of the fabric of what I am about professionally.

10
On the Record? Off the Record?

When attorneys want you to stop reporting during the course of a deposition, they will almost always give the command, "Off the record," or, "Go off the record," or something very similar. In most cases, opposing counsel will be silent. We reporters generally make the assumption that silence denotes agreement to go off the record, since lawyers as a rule are not shy about disputing *anything* they have a problem with.

If there is no agreement to go off the record among counsel, that is, if Lawyer A says, "Off the record" and Lawyer B instructs you to stay on the record, hornbook court reporting procedure demands that you keep reporting.

The courtesy of going off the record on demand extends even less to a witness. Sometimes a witness will crack a joke or even make a comment directly to you: "Don't take this down. My bladder's about to bust. When do I get a break?"

Do not stop the record at that point. Everything a witness says is testimony and is not to be tampered with in any way.

Stuck in the middle. Now on to the stickiest wicket of all. What happens if Lawyer A says to go off the record and Lawyer B says no; then Lawyer A insists that you stop? I have had instances where A looks right at me and says, "I'm not paying for this part of the record if you keep typing, so you better stop." What do you do?

Continue reporting anyway. When you graduate from school and gain the designation that your state confers on you, whether through certification testing or acquisition of a license, you are an officer of the court, just like the clerk, the judge, and yes, the attorneys. Review the Code of Ethics before you take your first assignment. You are obligated to follow the ethical mandates of your profession.

You can not be biased toward one side or the other, or even appear to be so, no matter who is paying the bill. Attorneys know this, but sometimes an acrimonious proceeding can test the limits of their patience. But do not be intimidated. Hold your ground.

If there is a lot of sniping back and forth between counsel, chances are when they calm down, they may turn to you and request that you strike all that foolishness. If only Lawyer A makes the request and B and C are silent, make a point of asking, "Counsel, do you all agree?" Then you can strike the specific portion.

When in court, however, *nothing* is stricken. Sometimes inappropriate comments made in the course of a jury or bench trial can render a proceeding appealable. Your choice to be a court reporter comes with it the responsibility to uphold the basic tenets of our judicial system.

The deposition setup is both an accommodation to parties involved in a lawsuit as well as to the court to the extent that it does not have to take place at the courthouse, but can occur in the convenience of a law office, or even at the witness' home. Because the environment is a bit more informal than actual court, people tend to be more relaxed. That's great, but don't let that blur your distinct and unique obligations to the judicial system.

After all, at the beginning of a witness'

testimony, you ask the person to raise his or her right hand and solemnly swear or affirm to tell the truth. You don't say, "Do you think you'll tell the truth?" And the witness gets his first taste of the formality and gravity of this legal proceeding from you. Their answer to you during the oath is a commitment made under penalty of perjury. "I do," or, "I will" is the response, not, "I think so," or, "We'll see how it goes."

Your profession is not just a nicely paid series of fun and interesting adventures; it is also a serious and significant contribution to the American way of life.

11
Read or Waive?

You may hear variations of the question above either at the beginning of a deposition or at the very end. "Are you reserving signature?" is another way to ask the same thing.

What the attorney is asking the witness, or sometimes asking the witness' attorney, is whether the guy on the hot seat wants to review the prepared transcript and sign something called a jurat indicating that he has actually read it over. If the defending attorney doesn't feel that the terminology was that complicated, she will often recommend that the witness waive signature, and the original of the deposition will be sent directly to the questioning attorney for filing with the court, if he so chooses.

When reserving signature, the witness signs the jurat under penalty of perjury, swearing that he has reviewed the transcript and deemed it accurate but for errors, if any, that he notes on what is called an errata page. He indicates the pages and lines he feels warrant corrections, and his lawyer sends the transcript on to the questioning attorney.

This all happens after your deposition is over. There are, however, a few simple things you need to know about this procedure. Keep reminding yourself, though, as you read through all these items, to make a list of what to do. After a few weeks, this will be second nature to you.

In the form book (see Chapter 7) you receive from your agency, there will be several different kinds of certificates that can be attached to the end of your finished transcript. One certificate has verbiage that deals with a witness having declared that he waives the reading and signing. One certificate has a jurat and errata sheets attached to it in the file, so it is a simple matter of clicking on the correct file to attach to your deposition. One certificate is strictly for a deposition where the decision to read or waive reading was not discussed at all.

If the choice is to read, don't make up that the parties don't trust you and want to make sure you got everything. I've said it before: we are all human, and even after careful proofreading, mistakes can be made. I may have misheard a word or phrase because the endocrinologist expert was from India and his accent was very thick; or this may be a highly sensitive patent case and the attorneys want to make doubly sure that everything that was testified to was what the witness actually meant to say. Nerves can sometimes wreak havoc on the most prepared of deponents.

When you are finished with a deposition that is "a read," as the term is used, aside from including the read certificate and attached pages, you also need to indicate on your billing sheet that this job is a read. When you turn in your files, you must tell the production department where the read letter must go. That is a letter notifying the witness that the transcript has been prepared in a hardbound book, and he usually has 30 days to review it.

The read letter is almost always sent to the defending attorney. If the latter has ordered a copy of the transcript, the letter will accompany that lawyer's copy, and the witness reads the testimony at his lawyer's office, returning the original jurat pages only. If the result is an 0 plus one, and the opposing attorney does not order a copy, the read letter is still sent to him, but the witness is invited to review the transcript at the court reporter's office, since there is no copy available for him to read at his lawyer's place.

I have taken a few pages to explain what will become rote to you in very short order. Remember, it will take time to absorb all the information in this book. But it is very much like eating a 50-pound turkey, which you are fully capable of consuming – one bite at a time!

12
Thank You, Uncle Sam!

One of the blessings that we enjoy is the opportunity that has been afforded us by the Internal Revenue Service to write off expenses that have been incurred in the course of performing our duties as independent contractors. Even some reporters who work in court have the ability to take advantage of available deductions if they are engaged in transcript production out of the confines of their court office, in the evenings or on weekends.

While there are a goodly number of freelance reporters who are identified as employees of the agency they primarily work for, the majority of freelancers are independent contractors who receive either 1099 income or who are set up as S corporations or LLCs (limited liability companies).

I spent all four years of my undergraduate

college life avoiding taking the math course required for graduation of English majors. In my senior year, however, the requirement was dropped, and I joyously threw away my calculator. I therefore openly admit that I am ill-equipped to handle even the most elementary of accounting concepts. I humbly, and wisely, I might add, follow the conservative recommendations of my financial advisor.

That being said, I am pretty well practiced at providing the basic information to my accountants relating to what I spend during the year in the course of my work. I prefer to be a fully independent contractor, taking out my own taxes and sending them quarterly to the state and federal entities, and keeping track of my own expenses. It takes a little more work, but I feel more in control of my finances.

Being classified in the eyes of the Internal Revenue Service as an independent contractor or S corporation or LLC is not for everyone. My father-in-law shuddered at the idea that we never knew how much money we would net each week after expenses and taxes. Keeping track of health insurance, tax payments, and itemizing deductions may be way too much to handle at first, so don't feel that being an employee of an agency is a hindrance. In fact, it may give you some breathing room to decide at a less frantic pace which tax path to take.

Things like insurance for my court reporting equipment, maintenance costs of same, paper for printing proofing drafts, costs related to a home office, and other items, all are painstakingly recorded over the year and reduce the taxable gross profit of my business. I try to use only one personal credit card for my expenses, just for easy recordkeeping.

Contact your national organization for professional insurance quotes. They have an arm of the group which focuses on hand insurance, malpractice insurance, disability, and other insurance vehicles that are specific to the court reporter's needs, and usually at very competitive rates. If you hurt your hand or lose your voice as a result of what laypeople might consider a fairly mild medical condition or accident, your money stops. Don't be foolish and leave your precious skills exposed to risk.

Even if you make a relatively small amount your first year in business, do not overlook the vital importance of opening up a pension account. Again, your accountant will be able to advise you which financial instrument will work best for you, whether it is a straight IRA, a Roth IRA, or a simplified employee pension (SEP) plan. A small amount invested every year for twenty years or more will grow into a great little nest egg when you're ready to reduce your hours in the field.

I highly recommend that when you first begin to work as a reporter, and even as you are hurtling toward your final qualifying tests as a senior student, that you speak to a reporter who has been in the field for a while and ask them who their accountant is. It is much easier, although not essential, to be able to communicate with a financial professional who is already familiar with our unusual job. You can even call some of the larger agencies in town and ask them. Most will be happy to point you in the right direction.

One important financial rule for court reporters to follow is: Don't drive yourself crazy with worry if you have a slow week. The corollary of that is, don't put a fat down payment on a Rolls Royce if you score a fantastic week. Even reporters who derive some of their income from transcript orders in addition to their salary in court experience some variance in pay from month to month. For freelance reporters, it is vital not to fixate on the potential variation in income from one week to the next.

The summer and the end of the year tend to slow down, which gives us time to do more leisurely activities (whether we want to or not). Our paychecks start to look a bit sickly at these times, but don't worry. As long as you pace yourself during the busy time and put aside some funds for those leaner weeks, you'll be fine. It's very important to look at freelance court reporting from a yearly income perspective; otherwise you will live in a sort of manic state, bemoaning the skinny checks and celebrating the fat ones.

12
Do Unto Others

As pointed out in other chapters, there are lots of ways to demonstrate to yourself and others the high level of professionalism that you have attained in a relatively short period of time. I have a couple more suggestions that I think are interesting enough that they deserve their own section in the book.

Being a court reporter is something of a "lone wolf" occupation, in that you operate and depend upon yourself for the most part to get from the beginning of your assignment to the end products, a finished transcript and a nice check. You are the only court reporter in the room taking down verbal utterances for posterity; you go back to the privacy of your home office or back to a makeshift cubby at the reporting agency to transcribe.

By the very nature of our work, we are

relegated to quiet places to develop our craft. So it is essential that we reach out to each other for professional support.

Gathering at national and local conventions is a powerful tool for reaching out to others similarly situated. I encourage you to join these organizations and attend more than the requisite number of seminars to fulfill the yearly CEUs (continuing education units).

There are also other ways to create a rapport between yourself and other reporters. One starts right at the conclusion of your reporting assignment.

While you are still in the deposition room, you may overhear that more witnesses are planned to be examined in the near future. This was covered in a previous chapter, but there is something more you can do to round out your slowly developing reputation as the consummate professional.

Assuming that you are not specifically asked to return to report the next deposition(s), you nevertheless dutifully notify your office of the dates and times of same. Let your scheduler know at the same time that you will have a glossary available for the next reporter, to please provide you with his or her email as soon as they know who is taking it, and you will be happy to send that person a cover page, appearance page, and a list of the spellings you have already obtained.

In the situation where the future deposition will not take place for a number of weeks, your case information will already have been turned in, so the agency can simply forward that on to the next reporter without your having to do anything; but in the case of a deposition going on within a few days or a week, your input is vital, and very much appreciated. If you know that the proceeding is going on the next day and you are assigned elsewhere (after a while, you may have more than one request for you on the same day – what a wonderful problem to have!), it's helpful to the reporter following you to come into the conference room that you are about to leave, and delightedly discover that you have left your colleague not only a list of the spellings, but also another piece of paper with a seating chart just showing the configuration of the participants around the table.

Be sure to write boldly on the top of the pages you leave for the next reporter, the words "DO NOT REMOVE." That way the night cleanup crew will not discard your handiwork. If the deposition is taking place in another location, you won't be leaving your artwork behind, of course, but, as previously described, you will be able to let the agency know you are willing to provide the information directly.

This practice is not just applicable to freelance reporting. When I worked for a few years in a busy federal court in New York, there were several trials a week that could result in 250 to 300 pages of transcript per day. Some trials lasted a few months, several days each week. This automatically meant that more than one reporter would be assigned to the case. At the end of each trial day, we were expected to leave an update sheet at our courtroom desk with names and terms and even suggestions for shortcut codes to make our buddies' lives easier.

A one-stroke steno form (or for present voicewriters, a one-syllable code) for a polysyllabic phrase was often a godsend in a technical or fast-paced case. "Chronic obstructive pulmonary disease" is not something I want to write out phonetically two or three hundred times in a medical malpractice case. In steno, I would invent the one-stroke **KRUP** and not only be right on top of the testimony, but also reduce the stress on my hands by lowering the number of swipes I'd have to take at my machine.

There is a little variation of the practice of helping out the next guy that I enjoy doing which nets me nothing in the way of attorney requests for my specific services; and nothing in the way of kudos from my agency; in short, nothing tangible at all. What it does yield for me is the satisfaction that I have reached out to my fellow professional in a way that supports the concept of cooperation and camaraderie.

That was a grand, sweeping statement, wasn't it? It certainly felt good to make it. Now, here are the details behind this declaration.

When a non-client attorney informs me that he prefers to use his own court reporting service, I ask him if he happens to know who they are, if I might be able to contact them to provide a glossary of names and terms to his reporter. This has been met with more than a few raised eyebrows, as well as, I would avow, a new respect. After all, court reporting agencies are fierce competitors, and teamwork is generally limited to within our own companies. Why ask to contact what is essentially a rival operation?

If the attorney knows the name of his

reporter group (sometimes only his secretary or paralegal knows, and I gladly contact them), and she gives it to me, I call and ask to speak to the scheduler or office manager. I identify myself as the reporter on the "Smith" case with their client, Mr. Jones, and tell them I am aware that their client will schedule or has scheduled a deposition for a particular date and time. I tell them that I have a glossary of names and terms that their reporter is welcome to use, and I would be glad to email it to them. The email address is usually that of the scheduler and not of an individual reporter. The sound of surprise is evident in this rival agency rep's voice as well, but I rarely get a refusal.

In the big picture, you now see another reporter entering a conference room for a new job, but armed with the ammunition that will create a better professional experience for that person as well as everyone around that table. In the smaller yet not less important picture, I have earned the respect of another court reporting organization that in the future could spell opportunity for me. How? This is a relatively small vocational circle. You develop a reputation in many ways.

At some point you might determine you want to move from where you are to somewhere else, or you might, as a pure freelancer, wish to add another client to your roster, and you might be interested in contacting the agency that you assisted to see if there is a spot available. What a great opening you have created by reminding them that you contacted them in the past in this unusual and innovative way.

Being proactive about creating positive change in your professional environment will serve you well as you gain experience.

13
War Stories

Everyone in this business has experiences that range far from the expected. In fact, I will go so far as to declare that when you are anticipating the most mundane, routine day; when you adopt a blasé, no-surprises-here attitude toward your assignment; that's when the mythical Fates start laughing and swoop down to mess up your tranquility.

Some of the anecdotes I have in my arsenal are funny; some are a little scary; and some are just plain weird. What they all share is the distinction of being my own personal evidence that this is the most awesome job in the world!

I get nicely paid for being a fly on the wall in the most fascinating situations. Even the depositions that feel slow-moving and tedious in terms of content almost always have a saving grace. Whether on or off the record, the personalities of those attending frequently lend a dimension to your time with them that you would not get in any other line of work.

There is the actuary expert drone, who spends all day with statistics determining life expectancies, asking me at breaks to explain to him how my stuff works, because he just can not believe what a boring job I have!

There is the more frequent question of, "Do you actually listen to the content of what you're hearing?" If the answer would be no, that would *really* be boring!

At the end of a deposition, a witness is often asked if he wants to read and sign the transcript or if he waives reading and signing. After declaring he wants to review the transcript, the person has turned to me and said, "I'll just go to the restroom, and I'll start reading it when I come back." Hey, buddy, I'm fast, but I'm not *that* fast!

Every time I was handed a document and asked to mark it as an exhibit, the questioning attorney would start to speak. I had to interrupt her several times to make her aware my hands were off the steno machine and she had to wait until I slapped on the sticker and got back into position before the testimony could continue. I was losing patience. Granted, people can forget that we're even in the room with them, but this was getting ridiculous.

I waited until the first break and cornered her in the hallway. "Just give me a few seconds to mark the document and we'll be back in business. I only have two hands." She nodded in assent and apologized.

The very first time after the examination resumed that I was requested to sticker another exhibit, boom, her motormouth kicked right into gear. I tried hard to conceal my frustration, declaring in a slightly sterner voice than before, *"One moment, counsel."* She replied in a tone that reeked of patronizing sympathy, "Oh, I'm so sorry. I know you only have two hands. Let me help you."

Before I could fully react to the strangely worded response, the attorney tossed two lifelike rubber hands at me, the kind that most often emerge during Halloween. It scared me half to death. Apparently, everyone at the table had been in on the joke except me. Once the laughter (in which I now participated) died down, the lawyer explained, "I've always wanted to 'lend a hand' to my court reporters! You guys work so hard, and sometimes it seems like you need a few more limbs to keep up with me. So here they are!"

I didn't mind being set up like that as long as she promised not to continue her marking/talking routine for the rest of the depo. And happily for me, she kept that promise.

A protracted trial of several suspected Mafia mobsters translated into an order for transcript that had to be delivered within a few hours of the close of each day. That not only required a team of reporters to keep up with the volume in order to meet the deadlines, but there was the issue of how to handle payment of the several thousand dollars per week that would be accruing to us over the course of this proceeding.

Not wanting to wait to hit the various legal firms associated with the case with a six-figure invoice at the end of the three months, we came to a resolution. At the end of each week, the reporter who started the Friday testimony would receive payment of the previous Friday to Thursday transcript fees from representatives of all defendants. We already had an agreement in place with the United States Attorney's office, so there was no need for a special arrangement there.

I was the first Friday morning stenographer, and was not surprised when what seemed to be a fifty-foot hulk in a well-tailored suit approached me in open court and said, in his very best Brooklyn accent, "Hi, Maxyne. I'm Dominic. I got yer cash right heah." I tried to hide my astonishment as he pulled out of his trouser pocket, Hollywood-style, a thick roll of hundred-dollar bills. He peeled off enough green to cover that week's invoice, rounding the amount to the nearest hundred, and offered it to me with a terse smile. "That should keep ya til next week, honey. Say hi to Richie for me."

A pack of wolves could have comfortably made their den in my mouth, it had dropped open that far. First, the overt, Central Casting nature of the initial exchange was interesting, to say the least; but the fact that he knew not only my name but my court reporter husband's name just blew me away. The reporters never put their names on the transcript. Typists (this was pre-computer) simply placed initials in the upper left-hand margin of each page to help us distinguish my sections from another reporter's.

Attorneys might be familiar with some of the reporters from previous encounters, but this was the first time I had walked into that courtroom for that case. Besides, very few people outside of the reporters' office knew that Richie was not only my colleague but also my spouse.

By the time I had requested the US marshal to escort me two floors down to the safe to deposit the funds, I was a basket case. I was the poster child for paranoia, and I confided in the marshal what had transpired earlier that morning. The law enforcement professional reassured me that it was nothing, and that the "bag man" was just messing with me. Thankfully, I wasn't made an offer I couldn't refuse, and I thoroughly enjoyed working that trial.

In my present position, I have the opportunity of driving all over creation to report depositions. My assignments are not only in the metropolitan area, but also range into the suburbs and rural regions outside of Atlanta. I love the rich variety of scenery I travel through, as well as the contrasts in culture and lifestyle that I encounter.

One witness examination landed me in a tiny, rural Georgia town in the spring. Chrysanthemums, crepe myrtles, and peach blossoms crowded the front yards of the houses I passed. As I walked to the tiny town hall across the square from where I had parked, a few chickens were making their way along the sidewalk. This was a far cry from the 30-story tower in Atlanta I had worked in the day before. I am drawn to the potential adventures this job promises, and diversity in venue is part of that.

Apparently, the office out of which my agency's client practiced either could not accommodate all four of us, or his meeting room was already taken up by some other matter. At any rate, the oversized conference room in town hall, with its impressive 25-foot wooden table, was home to our little proceeding that day.

This case involved a grandmother suing to gain custody of her nine-year-old granddaughter. Grandma was alleging that her daughter, a single mom and resident of big, bad Atlanta, was an unfit parent. Mom pushed back on that notion, and so a lawsuit was born.

I erroneously assumed that this would be a "vanilla" deposition: mildly interesting, but no real surprises. Sometimes it's worthwhile getting out of bed in the morning just to be wrong.

The interrogation began with the usual questions: name, address, education, etc. Granny was a tiny, blue-haired member of the local garden club and an elder in her church. She was convinced that life in a small town is far superior to that in a big city, especially when it comes to raising a child.

She claimed that things were so safe in her corner of the world that no one ever locked their doors. "In fact," she continued, quite animated, "every night I back my car on up my driveway and two aliens hop in the back seat and throw a force field around my house. Nobody can get in or out 'til dawn!"

You could have heard a pin drop. I could not believe what I had just heard. Needless to say, the attorney representing this lively senior became somewhat pale and ashen. "Off the record," he announced.

"Not just yet. I have a few more things to ask," my client stated, his voice not revealing one iota of surprise at the information the witness had just provided. And we all know, based on a previous chapter, that if the attorneys voice disagreement with going off the record, the reporter stays on the record. Boy, this was going to be fun. Jerry Springer, eat your heart out!

This is how the rest of the transcript looked:

Q   What do you mean by "aliens"? Are they people from another country?

A   Of course not. They're from outer space.

Q   Well, how do you know they're aliens from outer space?

A   By their paper hats, their beak noses, and their gold dresses, of course.

MR. CLIENT: Okay, now we can go off the record.

MR. OTHER ATTORNEY: Thank you very, very, very much.

Needless to say, as Granny and her attorney made a hasty exit from the conference room, the latter mumbled something about withdrawing the lawsuit with prejudice (meaning it would not be reinstituted for any reason – who would have guessed that one?). With the deposition adjourned and the other party gone, I smiled at the questioner, and told him I assumed that he would not want this transcribed.

"Oh, no. You *must* get this to me. I want to frame it and hang it in my office!" I guess an alien sighting was something of a novelty to him.

We court reporters hear about everything else, so why not throw a story of a rural Klingon into the mix.

Dreams can be very powerful. They can be inspiring, strange, even frightening. More than once my nightmare had me standing in the middle of New York's bustling Grand Central Station in my pajamas while more appropriately dressed throngs of people rushed past, each casting disapproving glances my way. Those who are trained in dream interpretation might say that, among other things, I feel worried and fear being exposed. Well, one day my dream became a reality – so to speak.

Being willing to take on whatever assignment is presented to me, no matter how unorthodox or strange it seems, allows me to experience my professional life in a way that many of my peers do not; it creates marvelous learning that I would never ordinarily acquire; it fattens my paycheck beyond the norm; and most importantly, it exposes me to some really strange stuff.

A large international religious group was having its convention at an enclosed stadium in my town, and they wanted realtime streamed to the executive board members who were making presentations to the participants at the business sessions. The organizers also requested online streaming of my realtime to delegates in other countries. Since there were so many people attending, my realtime was also hooked into a giant video monitor so that those present in the audience could see my raw transcript as I hit the keys. That was the exposure part – there wasn't a rock in sight anywhere that I could hide under.

Here's the worry part of the "dream." Since there were mission leaders from all over the world coming up to the audience microphone to share stories with and ask questions of the board, the support staff were angels of mercy coming to my rescue, feeding me the spellings of all these unfathomable names. What they were unable to do is help me with some of the amazingly thick foreign accents, and I had to write what I thought I heard.

I had decided that everybody would be looking at that giant video screen, and if I goofed up, I was done for. I kept silently coaching myself to remember that after a short time, in non-legal proceedings, the novelty of realtime wears off, and laypeople pay very little attention to what I'm doing.

Not that fateful day.

A missionary delegate from an African nation approached the audience microphone clad in the brilliant colors of his country's attire. I prayed each time a foreign-sounding name appeared on the monitor that that person would be relatively fluent in English. To my joy, this gentleman, despite his thick, melodious accent, fit the bill – except for that one pesky little word.

He was proud to announce, "Our district's organization has been extremely successful in collecting" – well, something that I heard as -- "Jews." I knew it was a very odd construction, but in that moment, I couldn't imagine another word that would fit, and realtime demanded that I put *something* in that space. In those precious few seconds, I told myself that this was an evangelical organization, and perhaps, because English was not his first language, he simply phrased the act of winning nonbelievers over to his religion in that odd way.

No such luck.

Laughter slowly erupted like a stadium-wide wave at a football game, only this wave was an audible one. It reached its peak as board members on the raised stage realized the error on their screen and they, too, began to chuckle.

There were thousands laughing!

The actual word that I had misheard was "dues." This man's mission was in positive territory financially and he was very proud of it. Thankfully, everyone present took this reporting gaffe good-naturedly, and I was approached dozens of times during the following days of the event by countless people reminding me, with a smile, multiple variations of, "We don't collect Jewish people, we just convert them!"

I haven't had that Grand Central dream since. My next fear dream is showing up at a deposition without any of my equipment. I am working very hard to keep that just between me and my pillow.

There are tons of other stories that I have tucked away in my memory, most not as drastic as these. I wake up every working day looking forward to the adventures, big or small, that await me.

What could be better?

RESOURCES

National Court Reporters Association
        ncraonline.org
        800-272-6272

National Voice Writers Association
        nvra.org
        601-582-4345

Stenograph Corporation
        stenograph.com
        800-323-4247

Advantage Software
        eclipsecat.com
        800-800-1759

Depobook
        depobookproducts.com
        800-830.8885

Pengad, Inc.
        Pengad.com
        800-631-6989

Reporters Paper & Mfg. Co.
        Rpmco.com
        800-626-6313

NOTES

NOTES

www.ingramcontent.com/pod-product-compliance
Lightning Source LLC
Chambersburg PA
CBHW060612200326
41521CB00007B/755